AFTER LOSS

courage and healing through God's grace

Lynelle Watford

Rising Higher Gift Book Series

As a collection of thoughts and selected scriptures, read these pages slowly, ponder, and apply as needed. Let the words, like a slow rain, soak deep into your soul.

You may not have chronic rheumatoid arthritis, serious eyesight challenges, or the grief of losing a son to suicide as I do, but I trust these scriptures will minister to your heart as they do mine.

Lynelle Watford

Loss 101

Loss steamrolls its way into our lives. Decimates our world. Leaves our minds in a fog. Pain and confusion beyond comprehension slam into our beings.

Whether it was a relationship or a comfort ripped from our hearts, we suddenly realize how precious that existence was to us.

Walk with me as we journey through deep loss. As we navigate through the pitfalls of grief. As we choose courage and healing.

Be strong, and
let your heart take courage,
all you who wait for the LORD!
Psalm 31:24

Shock

Loss. Deep, devastating, all-encompassing loss.

It sucks you in, chews you up, and spits you out.

It blankets you in mind-numbing shock, yet torments you with shards of memories—images, words, and emotions.

It hurtles body, soul, and spirit through what you were never created to experience—or survive. Your mind freezes, unable to comprehend such enormity. Your emotions whirl from intense grief to anger to frustration to … nothingness. Your spirit struggles, in vain, to get a grip, to trust God.

You are on a journey. Every excruciating step, sometimes forward, sometimes back, leaves you gasping for breath. Looking for hope. Wondering if you can go on.

You want a way out. Now. But none exists. That realization may fuel rage, deliver you to despair, or engulf you with helplessness.

All seems lost. All, that is, except for Jesus.

Weeping may tarry for the night,
but joy comes with the morning.
Psalm 30:5

Jesus is our peace.
Jesus holds
our eternal destiny.
Jesus is our refuge.
Jesus loves us as
His special creation.
Jesus will never leave us.
Jesus is enough.
Jesus. Is.

Emotions, Emotions

Emotions whirl in times of loss. Sadness. Anger. Discouragement. Hopelessness. And on it goes.

The changes tire and confuse us. Feelings whip us about like dead leaves on a chilly November day. Will the day ever end to temporarily stop this emotional beating?

Emotions are valid, but they don't have to rule our lives. I know this in my head. Some days I believe it in my heart.

When emotions fling me about, I cling to God and His Word for all I am worth.

And do you know what? Emotions that had just tossed me across the room like a limp rag doll, slither away.

Fears fail, strivings cease,
anger melts, woes decrease,
when I trust—trust in You,
Lord God Jehovah.

Guilt is gone, dark departs,
sadness scurries, doubts dissolve,
when I trust—trust in You,
Lord God Jehovah.

Peace protects, love surrounds,
grace restores, contentment comes,
when I trust—trust in You,
Lord God Jehovah.

You keep him
in perfect peace
whose mind is stayed on you,
because he trusts in you.
Isaiah 26:3

Who redeems your life from ruin;
who crowns you with
loving-kindness and tender mercies;
Psalm 103:4 MKJV

Life Goes On

It can be infuriating. It can be healing.

Tummies need feeding. Socks need washing. Vehicles need gas.

Loss binds us to a moment in time while life grinds on.

Responsibilities force us out of bed and keep us interacting with others. Daily duties provide structure in our newly-decimated world.

After a loss, we need time alone. Our damaged emotions may need extra quiet or pampering. But we also need to stay in the stream of life.

One woman, abandoned by her husband with six children under her care, put it this way, "It's good that life has to go on. It is brutal and yet is God's grace."

It is God's lovingkindness that physical needs urge us to invest in life, errands force us to get out in fresh air, and duties compel us to make our body move.

Yes, it is God's grace. Grace for our healing.

Tears

Tears bathe my cheeks. My weeping is a window to my soul engulfed in grief. Waves of pain crest and break. How will I survive the suicide death of my son?

The loss, with all its hideous facts, scorches me. Like touching a hot stove, it can only be endured for a moment. I escape. Distraction. Diversion. Regain enough strength to confront reality.

Somewhere in the cycle of painful reality and blessed diversion, I look up. "O God, help me! I cannot do this."

I cling to His comforting arms, strong and eternal, awash in my tears.

> There are not enough tears to flow
> there are not enough flowers to grow
> there are not enough winds to blow
> to take away my grief.
>
> There are not enough days and years
> there are not enough cares and fears
> there are not enough silent years
> to remove your memory.
>
> There are not enough mountain peaks
> there are not enough rivers deep
> there are not enough enemies' feet
> to stay God's comforting arms.

The eternal God is your dwelling place,
and underneath
are the everlasting arms.
Deuteronomy 33:27

Struggle to Understand

"I just don't understand!"

I don't understand how it happened. And I certainly do not understand why. Our 20-year-old son's suicide death is beyond my comprehension.

In John 10, Jesus told a story about a sheepfold, a shepherd and his sheep, and a thief. The people did not understand the point.

Jesus approached His message from another angle, explaining Himself as the Good Shepherd.

One day Jesus, my Good Shepherd, ended my struggle to understand with this thought: "I don't have to."

In His time on earth, Jesus gravitated to the desperate, destitute, and debilitated with a heart of kindness.

I can trust a God like that. I can rest in His promises.

Now when the thought comes, "I just don't understand!" I remind myself, "But I don't have to."

Trust in the LORD with all your heart, and do not lean on your own understanding.
Proverbs 3:5

Jesus ended my struggle to understand with this thought: "I don't have to."

Pour & Lift

After discovering her infant son had cerebral palsy, Lisa grieved. "I closed every curtain and I mourned for about two days. And what I cried about was, I needed to mourn that I lost the normal baby."

In times of loss, God invites you to pour out your heart to Him. To express every hidden thought and feeling. To express the anger, frustrations, hopelessness, resentment, sadness, and all the rest.

After unburdening your heart, you need to fill it. To take a few minutes to let God lift you up. Contemplate a psalm. Sing a favorite praise song. Or listen to music rehearsing God's goodness and faithfulness. Let Him restore you and infuse you with courage.

Continuing her story, Lisa said, "After those two days, I opened every curtain and I opened my heart."

"And I chose to get up and praise God that day," said Lisa, concluding her narrative.

(From Focus on the Family broadcast, June 16, 2020, Overcoming the Obstacles of Cerebral Palsy (Part 1 of 2), Lisa Sexton, No Such Thing as Can't by Lisa and Tyler Sexton.)

Trust in him at all times, O people;
pour out your heart before him;
God is a refuge for us.
Psalm 62:8

Forgive,
and you will be forgiven
Luke 6:37

Blame Is Not a Game

Sometimes I was angry with anyone connected to the loss of my son. That included me. Hindsight revealed what I could have done to help prevent the loss and what others did and didn't do that contributed to the tragedy.

Over the years, I released blame. I forgave myself and others. I told myself I had done my best.

But before forgiveness came, there came a day I contemplated turning my back on God.

After all, He was responsible for the deep grief that consumed me. He could have prevented the storm that destroyed my son's life.

But He didn't.

In my anger, I thought, "If that's how He's going to treat me, I can just walk away!"

I considered. A fundamental change must ensue. No one to pray to, no absolute truth to rely on. I would betray myself and my deepest needs. Abandoning my faith would be spiritual, mental, and emotional suicide. To cut the cord would sever me from God and all I am since my life is interwoven with His.

The horror snatched me from the brink.

I still get angry with God sometimes. Even give Him the silent treatment. But I won't walk away. My life is entwined with His forever.

Marathon Endurance

My husband and sons were long distance runners—5K and 10K—not sprinters. The length of the run affected their training.

Grief is a marathon. To finish, endurance is required.

1. Attend to needs—physical, emotional, mental, social, and spiritual. This is not selfishness. Unless you stay in the race, you will not be there for others.

2. Dose your pain. Grieving gobbles energy. You need breaks. Enjoy healthy escapes for pleasure or projects. If your loss is the death of a loved one, it is not betraying that person to be happy. Sadness does not connect you to your loved one. Love does.

3. Choose courage. Resolve to be a survivor, not a victim. Decide to persevere in God's strength. Rest when you falter. Keep your eyes on the goal.

Focus on these areas in your race to the finish line. Jesus came to give us life abundant. And that may be best appreciated with the backdrop of pain and loss.

> Grief is a marathon.
> To finish,
> endurance is required.

I came that they may have life
and have it abundantly.
John 10:10

Unchanging God

Praise songs poured salt on my wounds. Testimonies of God's intervention swirled confusion in my mind. Exclamations of "God is so good!" following favorable prayer outcomes wounded my soul.

Crushing loss shook me to the core. Everything shifted--down to bedrock values and faith.

Could a good God have allowed this devastating loss? I wondered.

It didn't make sense. My loss would not be dismissed with platitudes, for crushing reality wrenched each breath. That led me to put God's goodness on trial.

Yet I didn't want to live in anger and bitterness.

My theology—my faith—should not change based on my circumstances, I reasoned.

I decided to trust God is good, even when life turns dark. Like the child who may not understand the good intentions of loving parents, I could not understand God's ways. But I chose to accept them.

My soul settled with healing. And, again, I offered praise and enjoyed the testimonies of others.

You are good and do good; teach me your statutes. Psalm 119:68

One Word

Stunned by loss, you may be unable to do the simplest tasks—make a sandwich, pay your utility bill, or set your alarm.

Your once-quick mind is reduced to numbness and confusion.

Talking is difficult. Answers to questions are often, "I don't know." Fully formed prayers are elusive.

But you can always whisper, "Jesus." Simple. One word. A cry from the heart.

"Jesus."

With compassion and tenderness, He hears. He sees your distress and suffering. He cares.

"Jesus." One word you need to remember.

> *Therefore God has highly exalted him and*
> *bestowed on him the name that is above every name...*
> Philippians 2:9

You can always whisper,
"Jesus."

Come to me,
all who labor
and are heavy laden,
and I will give you rest.
Matthew 11:28

Ambushed

Losses saunter in like Alzheimer's disease. Or strike like a stroke. Either way, we are not emotionally prepared whether loss is physical, financial, or relational.

We were not created to lose a loved one to death or our health to a chronic disease. Shock clutches us in early seasons of grief.

In emotional shock, logic is meaningless. Even faith may be hollow. In medical shock, the top priority is treating the physical system. In emotional shock, caring for both the emotional and physical must be priorities.

Sleep. Eat. Rest. Repeat.

In time, we heal. Even then, expect ambushes. Events, songs, or objects may trigger an overwhelming sense of loss. In his presentation, "Tremors of Life: Ministering at a Time of Loss, Crisis, and Trauma," Dr. Norm Wright explained he still gets ambushed after 27 years since his son's death. "I would rather have that happen than be numb," Wright commented.

> In emotional shock, caring for both the emotional and physical must be priorities.

Staircase Out

Stories, movies, and books present conflicts, then resolutions. But real life isn't like that ... unless we wait long enough.

One devotional I read was different. Death left a hole. No more family pictures. I expected to read of healing, moving ahead. But it wasn't there. Only hope that next year they could stomach a family photo.

I was left hanging, surprised. Then validated.

This is real life. Problems don't resolve within an 80,000-word novel or 30-minute television segment. We're often left hanging. Maybe for the rest of our days.

In the meantime, how can we move toward healing?

Thankfulness. For the little, everyday things. For the journey. That we once had something precious, even though it was lost.

When I gave thanks for the loss of our son—an 'although-I-don't-feel-it-but-will-do-it-by-faith thanks'—I took a big step toward healing.

With each "Thank you, Lord," another stair-step forms. My heart heals a bit more.

In everything give thanks. I Thessalonians 5:18 KJV

Expressions of thanks,
offered by faith,
become the stairs
that lead us
ever closer to healing.

Splendid Scars

I have several. On my left hip and right knee, for repairs. On my abdomen, twice cut to remove two baby boys. Opened three more times to save my life. Those are the physical, unsightly ones.

Emotional wounds take more time and attention to heal. Loss inflicts crippling wounds to our souls. Healing comes through renewing our minds through God's Word, yielding our wills to His, and restoring our emotional health through the affirmation of God and others.

Healing produces scars. Scars are good. They show where others ministered, and hands of a loving God carried through loss. They reveal personal growth in courage and faith.

When an expensive ceramic vase breaks, it can be repaired with the art of kintsugi—mending the broken places with gold. The result is a more valuable and beautiful object with a unique history.

When our lives are fractured through loss, God the Master Artist can mend the fragmented places with spiritual treasures. He can bring about a greater beauty through our unique story.

This is your healing time.

He heals the brokenhearted and binds up their wounds.
Psalm 147:3

Beautiful Change

Gains and losses. We welcome happy moments—graduations, marriages, births, new possessions. And losses? They crash through crafted barriers, leaving gaping wounds.

But it's through losses I become more like Jesus.

It is in deep pain I begin to grasp the delusion of self-sufficiency. I encounter the place where I am not in control despite using resources that pulled me through in the past. A brick wall severs all options except the best one—to look up.

And so, I yield. Turn to God. Let Him decide what tomorrow looks like.

I whisper a prayer, "Please give me grace to trust You in this hard thing."

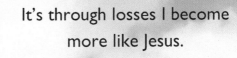

It's through losses I become
more like Jesus.

The LORD is my strength and my shield;
in him my heart trusts, and I am helped;
my heart exults, and with my song
I give thanks to him.
Psalm 28:7

Esther Stanard, Founder,
Miscarriage Matters

> *When you go through deep waters,*
> *I will be with you.*
> Isaiah 43:2 NLT

mymiscarriagematters.org

Find Meaning

Although she was a successful bank executive, Esther longed for a family. After twelve years of infertility, she was pregnant—with twins!

"I was so over the moon," Esther remembers.

But elation turned to sorrow after a double miscarriage.

Because Esther was unable to locate the one-on-one support she desired, she formed Miscarriage Matters. Volunteers offer support and compassion to parents around the world after miscarriage and stillbirth. Through a variety of internet-based resources in both English and Spanish, moms and dads connect with each other and with mentors.

With God's help, Esther and her team obey Christ's command to treat others as they would have wanted to be treated. "Helping others through Miscarriage Matters has helped me heal more than anything else," says Esther.

While you may not form an organization, in time, your loss may lead you to show compassion to others in adversity. In doing so, you will help others on their healing journey. You will help bring healing to yourself.

End of Fear's Domain

Fear nipped at my heels. And the clincher? It used truth to stay close, to remind me tragedy could again pierce my heart. The unthinkable had happened once. It could happen again.

I knew God did not want me to live in fear. But nothing seemed to stop the anxiety, the dark cloud.

Until. One winter night I pondered the phrase from Psalm 1:3, "He is like a tree planted ..." I pictured God embedding me in the circumstances He knew would be best for me. With tender hands. With forethought so all my needs would be met.

Peace settled and soothed like a luxurious blanket. Yes, I can trust this kind of God. Trust Him to plant me, to care for me.

Truth, befriended and pursued, sank deep into my soul. I knew I was safe. If tragedy pierced again, God would carry me as He had done before.

And fear? It had no choice but to scuttle away.

With hands of love God planted me
in a good place and will bring blessings from my life.

In this season of your life with your hopes, fears, and heartaches
God has put you right where He wants you
and has provided everything you need to prosper.

He is like a tree
planted by streams of water
that yields its fruit in its season,
and its leaf does not wither.
In all that he does, he prospers.
Psalm 1:3

Whatever you have lost,
much remains.

What Remains

In a quiet moment, I consider my future. Hands ravaged by fifty years of rheumatoid arthritis. Fast-deteriorating retinas. Do they spell a life of extreme disability?

My stomach feels sick. How can I accomplish anything while shielding my hands from pressure or movement? How can I navigate with dimmed and blurred vision?

You have your voice.

A voice is something. It speaks words of encouragement and truth. It gives life. That would be a way to live—to share what God teaches me through loss.

What have you lost? A career? A spouse? A future? Good health? Finances? A baby?

Your loss is great but know that whatever you have lost, much remains. Perhaps you have hands that can do something loving for another hurting person. Maybe you have eyes to admire God's creation and praise Him. Or perhaps you have a voice. A voice to acknowledge God is good and to bless others.

A gentle tongue is a tree of life.
Proverbs 15:4

New World

When 2020 dawned, few could imagine what the year would hold. A deadly virus. Face masks. Social distancing. Remote contact.

Our world changed, but it was difficult to envision that change before it happened.

Likewise, it is difficult to imagine sorrows erased when we are in misery. Life may be filled with torment of an abducted relationship through rejection or death. Or physical agony. Or the emotional pain of fear of the future or regrets of the past.

For the child of God, one day total joy in God's presence will replace suffering. It is almost too difficult to believe. Yet God's Word promises exactly that.

The difficulty you face is real, but so is your eternity with God. Be encouraged with the future reality. Listen to songs or read scriptures about heaven. Imagine Jesus preparing a place for you right now.

Had we known ahead of time, we would not have looked forward to living in a global pandemic. But it is delightful to consider our heavenly home. A place free from affliction and loss and full of joy. A new world.

For this light momentary affliction is preparing for us
an eternal weight of glory beyond all comparison,
as we look not to the things that are seen
but to the things that are unseen.
For the things that are seen are transient,
but the things that are unseen are eternal.
2 Corinthians 4:17-18

If you enjoyed this book, please leave a review on Amazon.com. Your review will help more people find encouragement through this book. Thank you.

Topics in this book:

Shock; Emotions, Emotions; Life Goes On; Tears; Struggle to Understand; Pour & Lift; Blame Is Not a Game; Marathon Endurance; One Word; Ambushed; Unchanging God; Staircase Out; Splendid Scars; Beautiful Change; Find Meaning; End of Fear's Domain; What Remains; New World.

Other books in the Rising Higher Gift Book Series:

Finding Hope: a journey of faith through uncertain times
Never Alone: gentle reminders of God's presence and love

Net proceeds from the sale of this series will be donated to the support of orphans through GlobalFingerprints.

More books by Lynelle Watford are available at ForeverWaters.com:

Out of the Ashes: Hope
Out of the Desert: Refreshment
Out of the Storm: Peace
Waters of Refreshment
Soul Pursuit: The Busy Person's Guide to Biblical Meditation
  (Soul Pursuit is also available on Amazon.com)

Subscribe to Lynelle Watford's blog at ForeverWaters.com.

Made in the USA
Monee, IL
14 February 2021

59394569R00026